THE GOOD DRUG AND THE BAD DRUG

THE
GOOD DRUG
AND THE
BAD DRUG

BY
JOHN S. MARR, M.D.

WITH ILLUSTRATIONS BY
LYNN SWEAT

Published by
M. EVANS AND COMPANY, INC., New York
and distributed in association with
J. B. Lippincott Company, Philadelphia and New York

ABOUT THIS BOOK

Here is a book that takes you on two complete trips through your body. First with a good drug and then with a bad one. The good drug is medicine that comes from a doctor. By following its course through your body, you get to understand what medicine does to every part of you. The bad drug is "dope." The second journey makes clear in every way how your body and mind react to a bad drug.

The author of this book is a doctor in a large city hospital where he has watched the effect of good drugs and bad drugs on hundreds of patients of every age. The artist whose three-color pictures help make the text so clear, has worked on other science books that have proved popular.

Because THE GOOD DRUG AND THE BAD DRUG is science and not a sermon, it will help you make up your own mind about the drug scene.

A good drug is given to you by a doctor when you are sick. The doctor can tell you what part of you is sick and what kind of drug you should take to become well again.

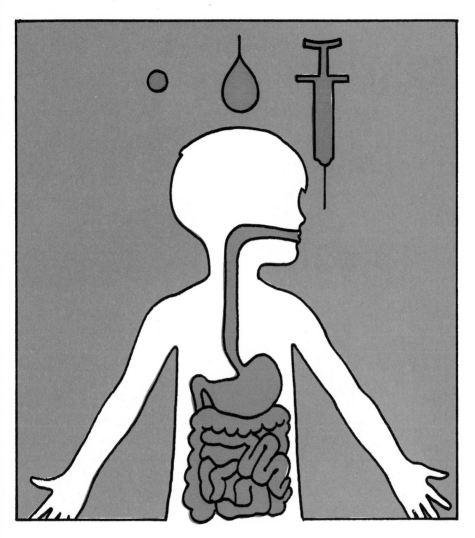

A good drug can be a pill, a syrup or an injection. When you swallow a pill or a syrup, it goes from your mouth, down your esophagus to your stomach. The drug dissolves and mixes in your stomach fluids. The drug is now ready to be

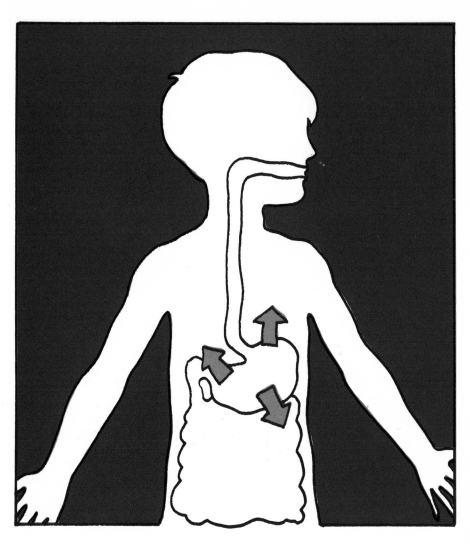

used by your body.

Like the food you eat, the good drug that has mixed with your stomach fluids is absorbed into the lining of your

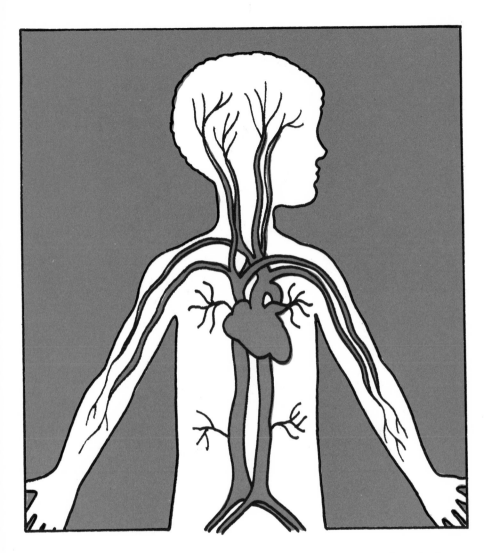

stomach. It is now ready to be put into your circulation. Circulation is a word that describes how your blood spreads throughout your body. When the good drug crosses from your stomach lining into your circulation it becomes mixed

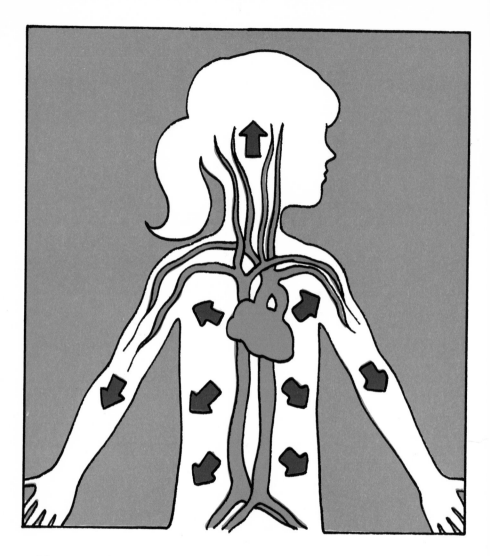

with your blood. Your circulation (or bloodstream) depends on three parts which are connected to each other: your heart which acts like a pump; your arteries which act like pipes that carry blood away from your heart when it pumps; and your veins which act like pipes that carry blood from the distant parts of your body to your heart.

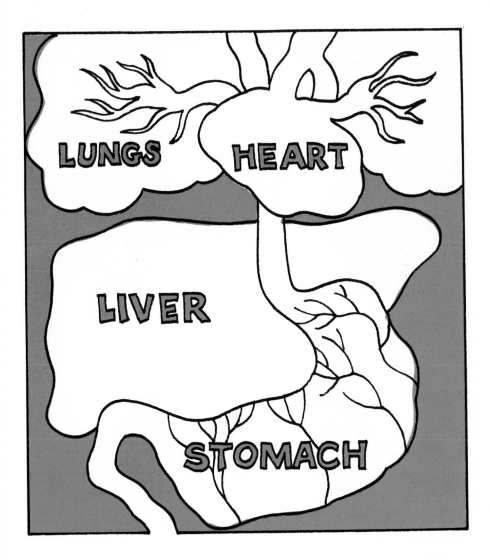

Once the good drug goes through the stomach lining, it is picked up by your stomach veins. The stomach veins carry the drug to your liver and then to your heart. Your heart then pumps the blood with the good drug mixed in it to your lungs which are full of the air you breathe. Here the blood picks up oxygen then goes back to your heart. Now the heart

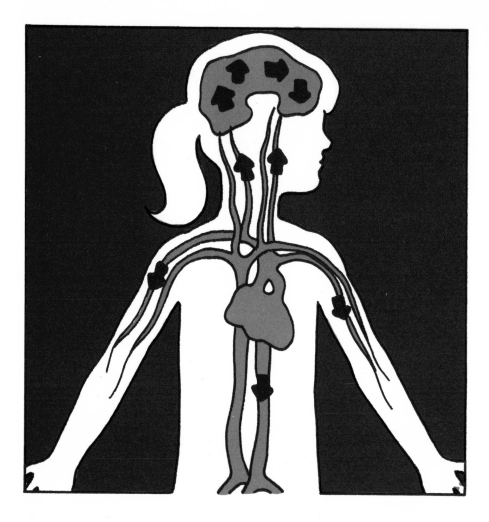

pumps the blood mixed with the good drug and oxygen out into arteries. The blood goes out of the heart in arteries to every part of your body: your brain, your eyes, your lungs, your heart, your arms and legs, your skin. The blood mixed with the good drug will be in the arteries that go to the place where you are sick.

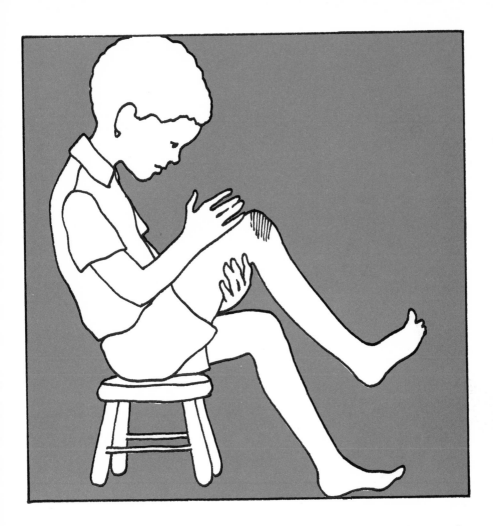

The part of you that is sick is usually red, swollen, hot and painful. If it is on your skin, you can see the redness, touch the swelling and feel the warmth and pain. If the part of you that is sick is inside your body, you cannot see the redness or touch the swelling, but you can feel the pain and warmth.

The reason the doctor takes your temperature is to see how hot you are. Everyone has the same temperature when he is healthy. When you become sick, your temperature is higher than normal. Sweating a lot when you have not been

running or working hard usually means your temperature is higher than normal. A high temperature usually means that you are sick.

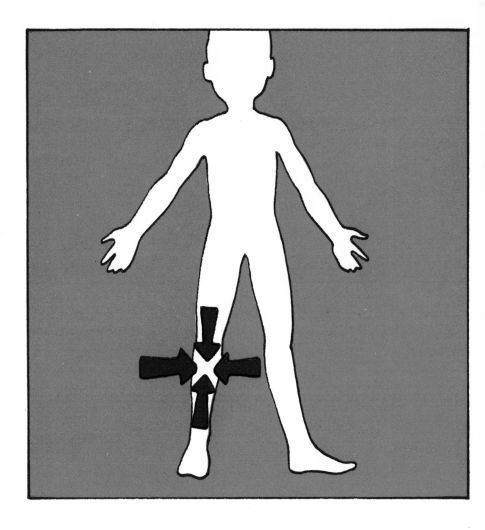

The good drug will arrive at the place that is causing your sickness. It will help your body fight the sickness. Your body can fight a sickness by itself, but a good drug helps your body fight the sickness faster. The redness is really caused by your body forcing extra blood into the area of sickness. Many small arteries swell to let more blood bathe the sick

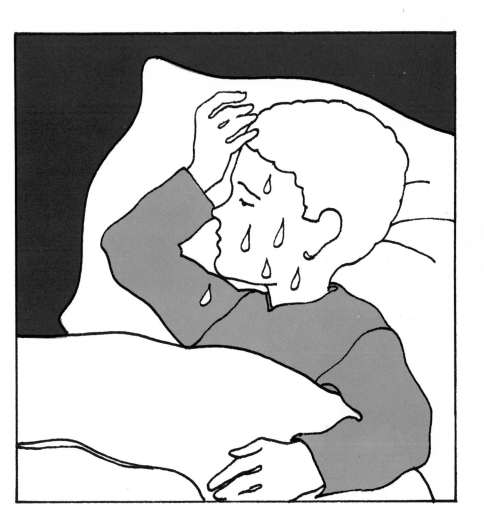

area. The swelling is caused by the extra blood fighting off the sickness. The pain is caused by the swelling pushing against nerves. The warmth and high temperature are caused by the sickness and your body fighting each other. Sweating is a way your body can lower your temperature. When the sweat evaporates, it lowers the temperature of your skin.

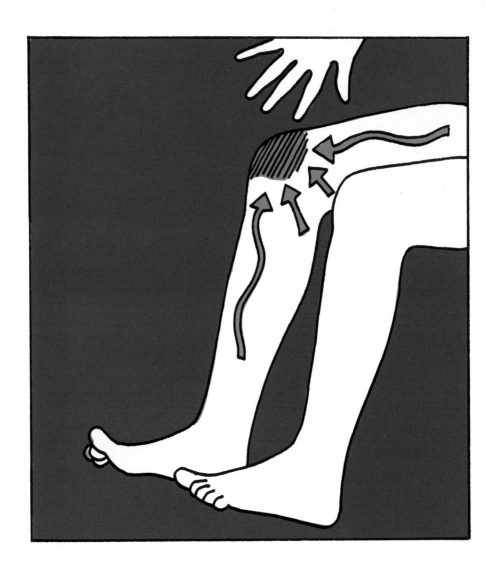

Usually the sick part is caused by germs. This is called an infection. When the germs start to grow in a part of you, your body begins to fight them. That is when the redness begins. A good drug gets inside the germs and prevents them

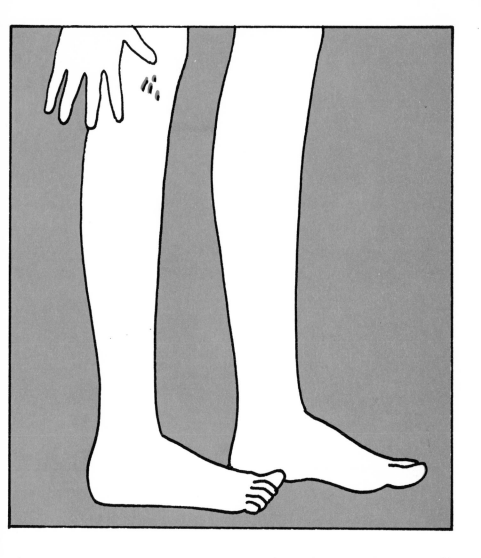

from growing larger. It weakens them by punching small holes in them so that they can be killed by the body more easily. As the germs die, the area of infection slowly becomes smaller. The redness begins to disappear. The swelling goes

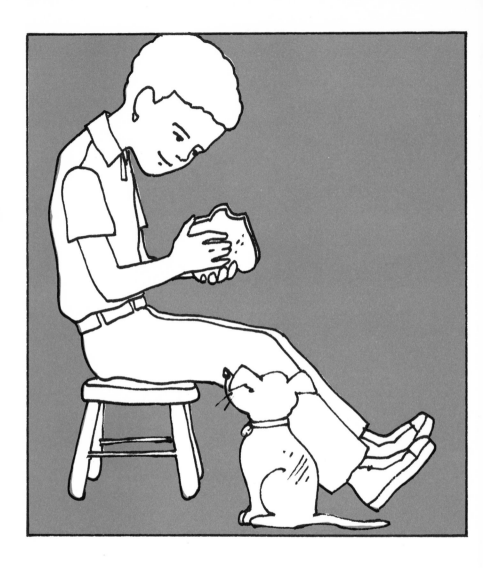

down, the pain disappears and your temperature returns to normal. Because your temperature is back to normal, you stop sweating. The weakness you felt when you were sick disappears. You become hungry and begin to eat. You feel

stronger because the energy that was being used to cure the infection can now be used to walk, run and play games.

When the doctor wants faster action from the good drug he will give it to you by injection. In an injection the good

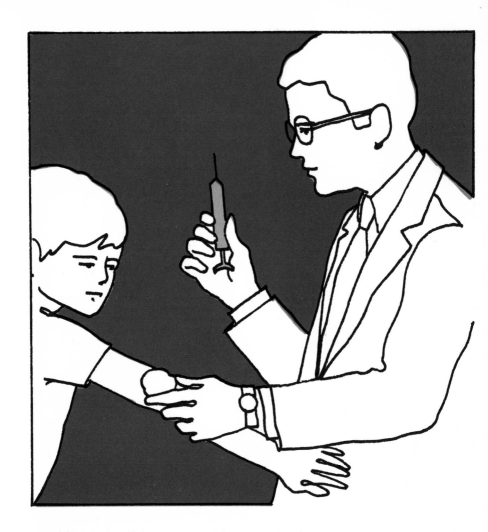

drug is already in liquid form and ready to be used by your body. It gets into a vein. It does not go to your stomach and so it goes into your bloodstream and to the sick part of your body much faster.

A good drug is called medicine. The doctor is the only person who can decide whether you should take a drug or

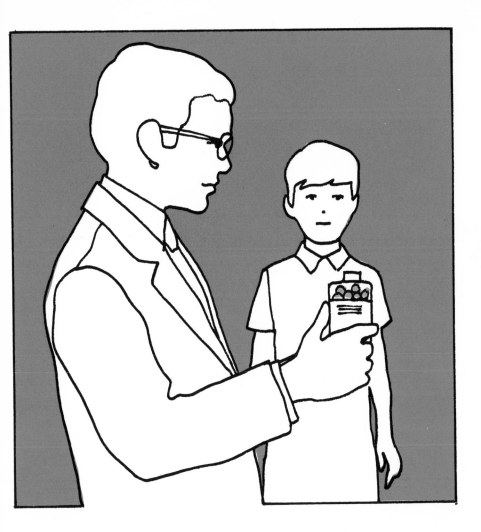

not. A good drug must be taken in certain amounts, in certain ways, and for a certain number of days. If it is taken the wrong way or if too much is taken, it might not do any good at all and it could even hurt you. Part of being a good drug is having it come with the right instructions.

A bad drug is given to you by someone when you are not sick, but are feeling normal and healthy. The person could be a stranger or, worse, even a friend of yours. The person might tell you that the bad drug will be fun. The person might tell you that it won't hurt you. That person is wrong. Some-

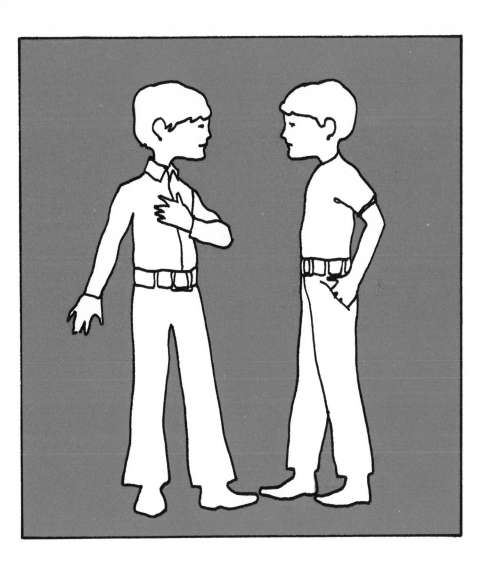

times he really knows that he is lying. Most of the time he doesn't know any better.

The person will say that he has taken the bad drug and that it made him feel good. He won't tell you the reason why he takes the bad drug. He might be a show-off or he might

be trying to be different. Or he might be an addict and not know it. An addict is a person who needs a bad drug like a normal person needs food. If he cannot get enough of the bad drug, he will get very sick. He has to take the bad drug—

not to feel good—but to keep himself from becoming very sick. The bad drugs cost a great deal of money. Some people must sell bad drugs to other people in order to buy more bad drugs for themselves.

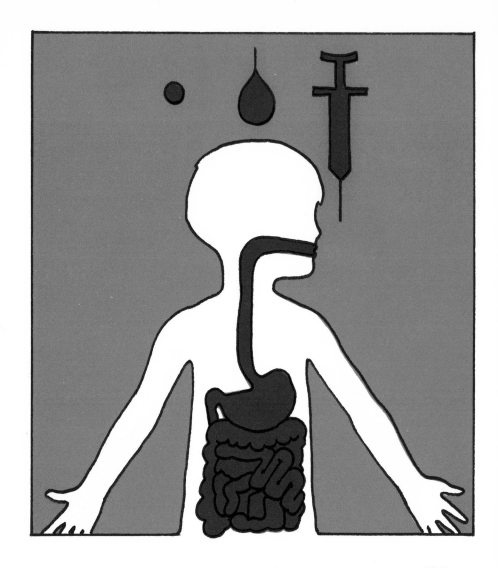

A bad drug can be a pill, a syrup or an injection. When you swallow a bad drug, it goes from your mouth, down your esophagus to your stomach. The drug mixes with your stomach fluids and is absorbed by the lining of your stomach.

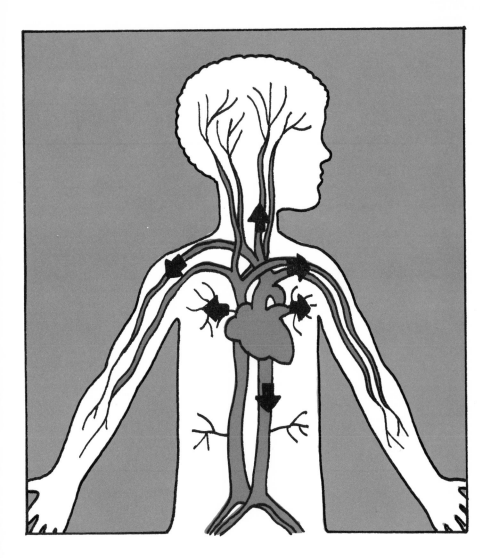

The veins of the stomach pick up the bad drug and carry it in your circulation to your heart.

Your heart pumps the bad drug to your lungs, back into your heart, then out through the arteries of your body to

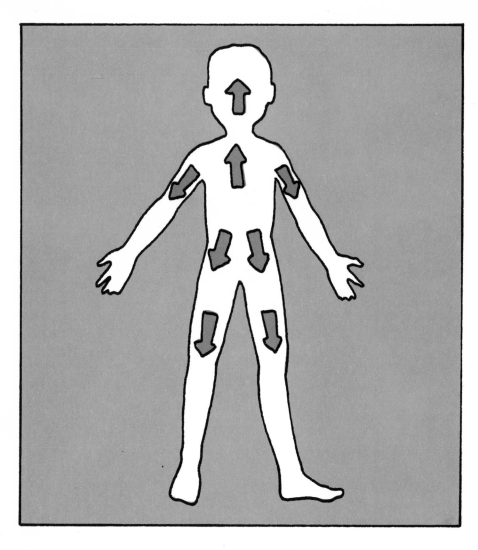

every part of you. The bad drug goes everywhere: your brain, your eyes, your lungs, your heart, your arms and legs, your skin. The bad drug changes your body. Here is how one bad drug works.

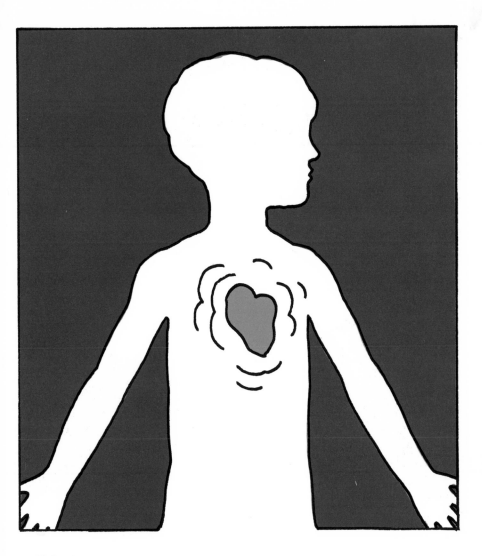

When the bad drug circulates through your heart, it triggers your heart to beat faster. Your heart squeezes harder every time it beats. Your heart beats just as fast as when you have an infection or after you run a mile. You can feel it

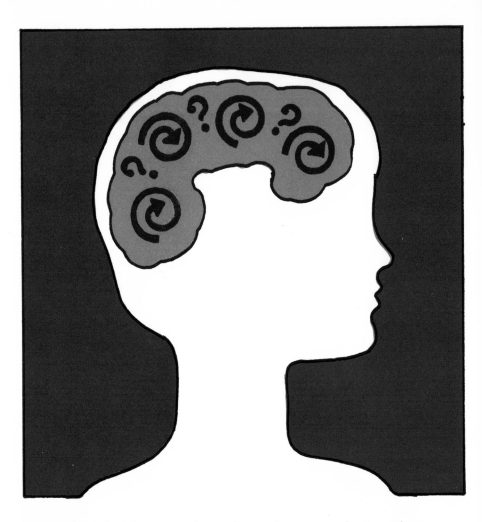

pounding inside your chest. Sometimes you feel as if you can hear it beating. You can feel the arteries in your wrists pulsing hard because your heart is beating so hard and so fast.

The bad drug goes to your brain. It makes the brain work not only fast, but too fast. You think of so many things in one second that you become confused. You cannot do any-

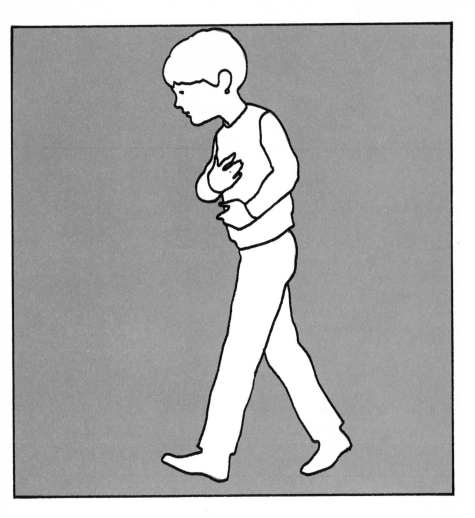

thing because your brain is telling you to do so many things at one time.

The bad drug makes you lose your appetite. You forget to eat your lunch or dinner. You don't feel hungry even though your body really is hungry. Your stomach growls for food. Your intestines don't have any food in them. They

sometimes can go into spasms because there is no food in them to digest and this gives you a horrible pain.

The bad drug goes to your muscles. Your muscles feel bigger and stronger, but they are really the same as they have always been. You feel as if you could pick up anything or that you could run forever. If you try to pick up something

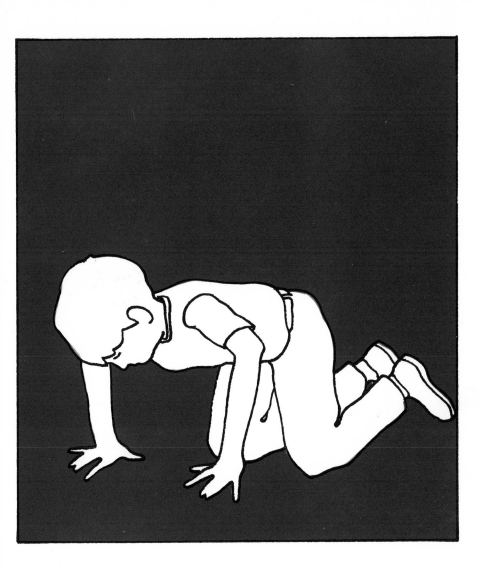

too heavy, you could hurt yourself. If you try to run for too long and too fast, you could exhaust your body completely. You would feel the way a man does immediately after running a marathon race.

The bad drug goes to your skin. It can cause your skin to sweat a lot as if you have a fever.

As your body begins to get rid of the bad drug, you begin to feel worse. Your brain is tired from all the different thoughts it has been sending out. Although you feel tired, your brain and its thousands of thoughts keep you awake. You try to go to sleep, but you cannot. You begin to feel nervous. A small sound like a telephone ringing makes you

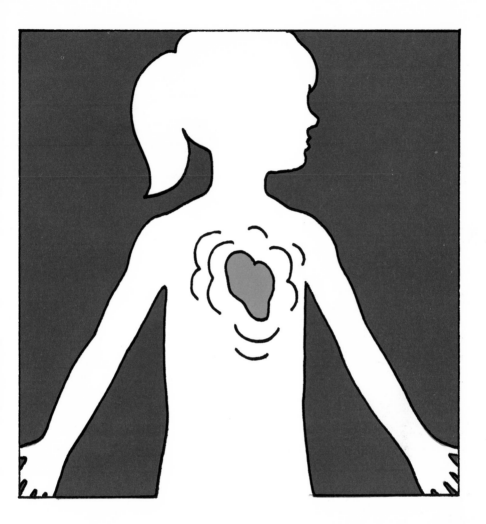

jumpy. You try to read a book or watch television, but you cannot concentrate on anything. Everything distracts you.

Your heart is still beating hard and fast even if you are sitting quietly. You can still feel every beat and the arteries are still pulsing. Your stomach still growls and hurts. Some people do not like these signs. You would not like the nerv-

ousness, pounding heart, sweaty skin and growly stomach. This is what happens when the bad drug begins to wear off. Although you would feel normal again after the bad drug wore off entirely, you might not be able to wait. So you

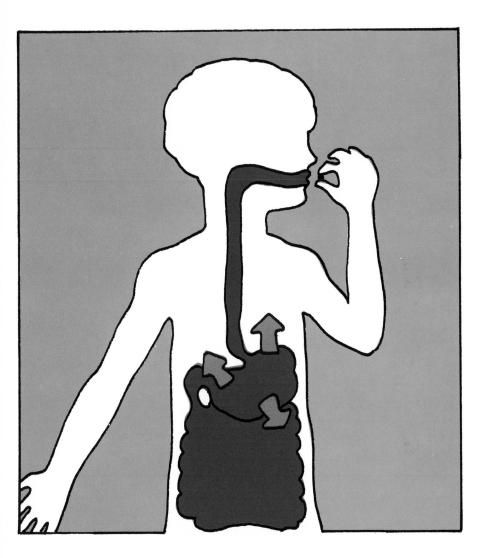

might take another dose of the bad drug in order to feel superstrong and able to get things done again. The second time you take the drug, it takes more to make you feel the same way. But no matter how much drug you take, it will

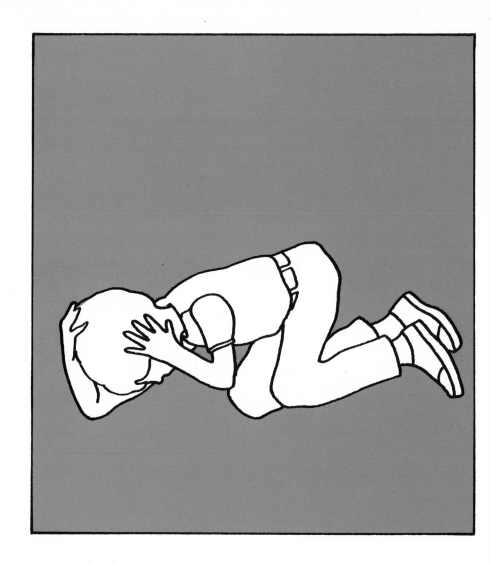

wear off. The more bad drug you take, the worse the feelings you will have when it begins to wear off. People who get in the habit of taking more bad drugs all the time are called addicts. Bad drugs are called dope.

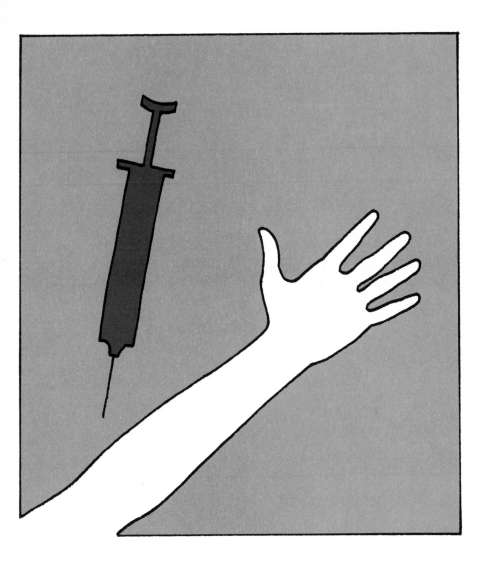

A lot of the dope you hear about is taken by injection. Most of the people described as addicts take their dope by injection. There are many reasons why injections of bad drugs are dangerous. One reason is that the needle is not

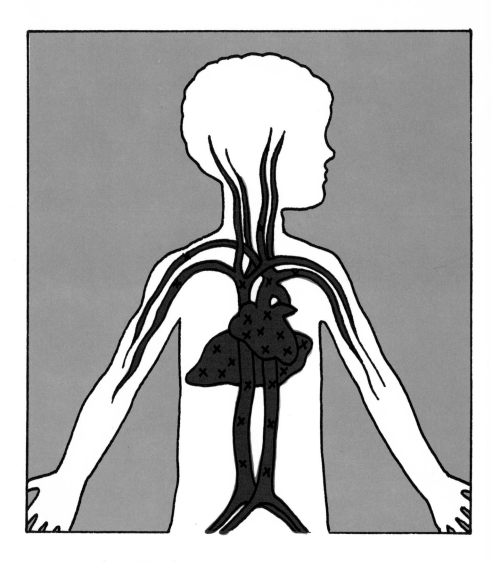

new and clean like the needle a doctor would use. The needle will have germs on it, and when you inject the bad drug into your circulation, the germs are carried into your body too. Some germs hurt your liver. Some germs hurt your heart.

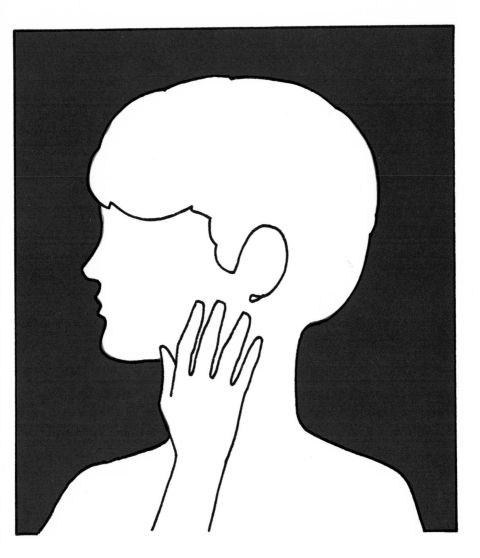

Some germs give you lockjaw. All of them can cause permanent damage to your body. Another reason that injecting a bad drug is dangerous is that you might inject too much of it at one time. Here is what happens when you inject one kind of bad drug.

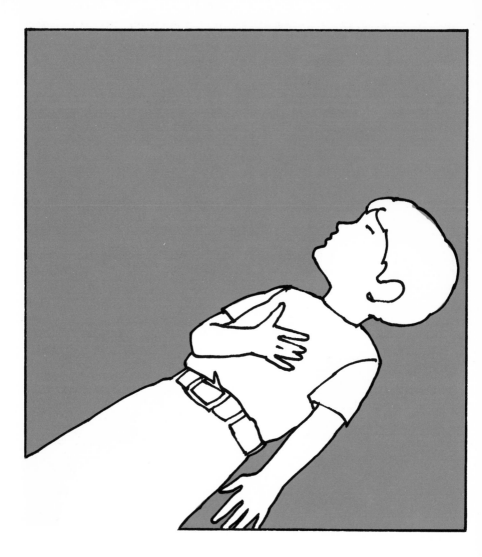

As the drug gets into your circulation, you feel funny. Then as it spreads to every part of your body, you feel very tired and weak. You lie down and funny dreams confuse you. You cannot stand up or talk. As more and more drug spreads through your body, it affects your brain. You feel as if you

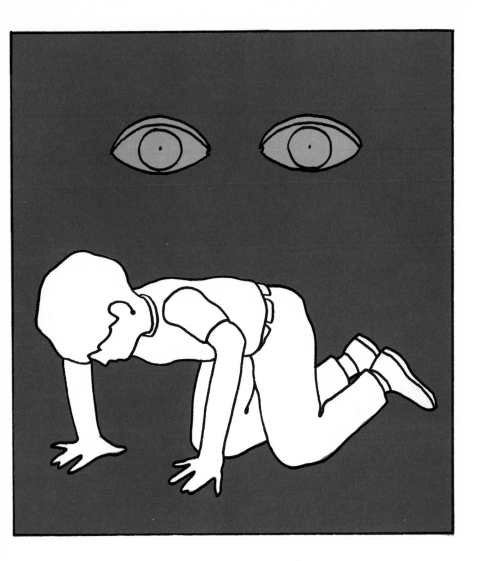

cannot stay awake. You cannot even open your eyes. You can fall down and become unconscious. The drug causes the pupils in your eyes to become tiny. The pumping action of your heart slows down. Your body does not get blood and

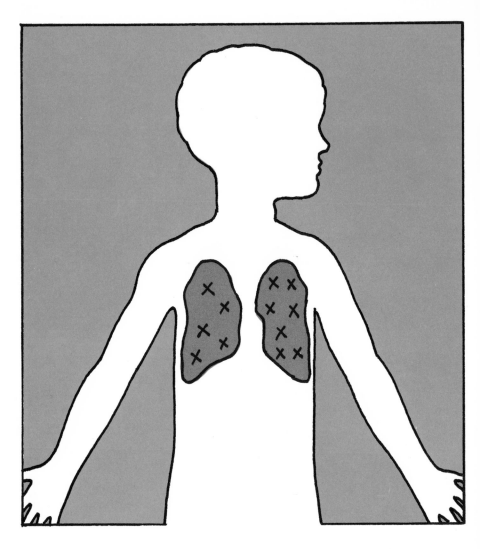

oxygen because the pump is too slow and weak. Your lungs slowly stop breathing. No oxygen gets into your lungs or bloodstream. Your fingers, tongue and lips turn blue because there is no oxygen being pumped into them. If there is

enough bad drug injected into you, you will stop breathing completely and you will die. Taking too much of a bad drug is called an overdose. Since injections of bad drugs never come from a doctor who can measure them carefully, overdoses are very common.

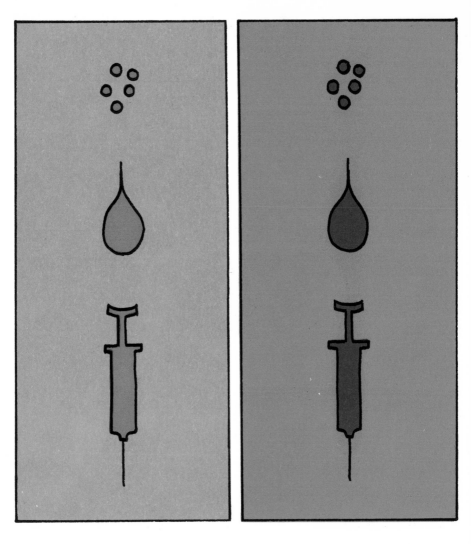

Since both medicine and dope come in the form of pills, syrups and injections, it is often difficult to tell them apart. Never take a drug without the directions of your doctor or your parents, because a bad drug can make a well person very sick and only a good drug can make a sick person well.